The
Green
Lunch
Box

The Green Lunch Box

Recipes that are good
for you and the planet

Becky Alexander

Illustrations by Sally Caulwell

Photography by Issy Croker

LAURENCE KING PUBLISHING

How to save the planet
in your lunch break

We're all thinking about climate change and want to make meaningful changes in our lives, but the advice on how to do this can sometimes feel overwhelming or confusing. We're also busy, and being more eco-friendly can be hard to incorporate into our lifestyles. Let's simplify things. You can make small, relatively easy changes that will make a difference, and you can do it in your lunch break.

Making your own lunch, even just once a week, will help reduce the tidal wave of single-use packaging that is being produced. We get through mountains of sandwich packets, salad boxes, soup pots and snack wrappers every single day in the UK alone.* Most of it is not, or cannot, be recycled and is transported to other countries or incinerated. We simply have to use less. Taking a lunch box to work is one way to reduce the amount of single-use plastic you buy.

Another way to help the planet is to reduce the amount of animal protein we eat, so everything in this book is vegan or vegetarian, making that a little easier for you.

Cutting back on the amount of meat you eat is the single most effective way to reduce your impact on the planet – ahead of cutting down on driving and flying. **

Do you prefer to buy seasonal and local produce? Well, most mass-produced lunches just don't have that flexibility. Manufacturers churn out the same salads and sandwiches, whatever the season, flying in ingredients, when we often have alternatives closer to home. If you buy seasonal food, get a veg box delivery, or grow your own – I hope you find some new ideas in here for how to use your veg. Mass-produced lunches also rarely contain high-welfare meat, fish and animal products. If you care about animal welfare, wise up to where your animal protein comes from.

The mark-up on mass-produced lunches means that you get better value for money making your own, too. You get to choose better quality ingredients and have much more control over what you're eating – a plant-based lunch is also a great way to incorporate healthier choices into your diet.

It is also quite easy to get stuck in a rut with lunch, and eat the same thing every week, whether you eat at work or at home. This book contains sixty easy, delicious, plant-based recipes, from summer salads to warming winter soups and hotpots, flavour-packed wraps and sandwiches, and snacks to keep you going between meetings. Whether you're eating at home or out and about, these recipes will save you time and money, and help reduce your impact on the planet.

Don't beat yourself up if not every lunch you eat is perfectly eco-friendly – small differences all add up to make a BIG difference. The lunchtime revolution starts here!

Shop and prep

Does making your own lunch sound like a time-consuming hassle? Let's face it, queuing up during your precious lunch break in a busy supermarket or deli isn't that quick or much fun anyway. It's more a case of how and where you spend your time. Why not start with making just one or two lunches a week; even that will help to cut down on packaging, and you might find you start to prefer it.

---

*On a global level, we produce 78 million tonnes of plastic packaging every year, with just 14 per cent getting recycled (www.nationalgeographic.com, August 2019).

**Author conclusion from paper by Dr M. Clark (The Oxford Martin School and Nuffield Department of Population Health) et al, Global Food System Emissions, *Science*, November 2020.

To help you get organized and maximize your time, you will spot the following symbols alongside recipes:

FF **Fridge forage.** When you need to work with whatever random things you've got.

5 **5 minutes.** Super-quick lunches. Ideal for when working at home.

LL **Love your leftovers.** Lunches that use up the most common leftovers.

NB **Night before**. Low-effort recipes that might be a bit rushed to make just before work.

W **Weekend.** Batch-cook recipes and advance prep that can be done when you have more time.

And here are a few tips for making lunch as effortless as possible:

1. **Stock up at the weekend** with cans of pulses and legumes, jars of olives, frozen vegetables, etc., so you always have something you can base lunch on. Having these precooked or store-cupboard staples to hand is key to making a green lunch box achievable.

2. **Try out a veg box delivery scheme.** They are so flexible now; you can skip things you don't like, pause deliveries when you're away, and order small, medium or large boxes. Try a scheme that includes supermarket rejects (ingredients that are considered to be the wrong size or are surplus) so you get plenty of variety, and not just lots of winter veg in the 'hunger' months. They are a great way to challenge yourself to eat veg that you don't always buy, and I have included ideas for some of the 'trickier' ingredients you might get in a box delivery.

3. **Source local produce.** Low food miles mean lower carbon emissions. Supermarkets often display green beans, apples and tomatoes that have been flown in right alongside home-grown produce, so read the labels carefully.

4. **Think local.** Importing food, such as avocados, is problematic. Think about ways of mixing it up a bit if you tend to buy a lot of imports. Peas, for example, are a good source of protein, and delicious with chilli and lime on toast (see page 96). Farm shops and markets are more likely to sell locally grown produce than supermarkets.

5. **Buy long-lasting fresh vegetables and fruits.** Radishes, spinach, peppers, carrots, parsnips, squash, etc. will last for ages, so are good options for end-of-week lunches.

6. **Mix and match.** If you don't have a certain ingredient or it's out of season, then have a go with something else. It's lunch, not restaurant cooking, so swap things around according to what you have.

7. **Try refilling.** Collect a few glass jars and head to a refill store or farmers' market stall for pulses, legumes, rice, pasta, grains, spices, nuts, dried fruit, chocolate, nutritional yeast, olive oil and much more. This is great if you only need a tiny amount of something or aren't sure if you will like it.

8. **Use fabric or string bags** when you buy your loose veg and fruit, or reuse plastic bags you already own as many times as you possibly can. Keep bags at work or in the car so you don't forget them. Paper bags are easier to recycle than plastic.

9. **Prep ahead.** Make a soup or roast some veg at the weekend and you are ahead of the game for later that week. Cook a small batch of dried pulses or beans, if you like. If you are always throwing out old ginger and garlic, get into the habit of chopping the remnants and putting them in the freezer. You can cook with them from frozen – one teaspoon is about the same as one clove of garlic or 1cm (½in) piece of ginger – or buy them pre-chopped in jars.

10. **Eco-friendly cooking tips.** You might not need to preheat the oven for as long as you think – the newer the oven, the quicker it's likely

to reach temperature. Roasting vegetables when the oven is on for something else is more eco-friendly than turning it on especially for lunch. All centigrade temperatures in the recipes are for an electric fan oven. Conversions for standard electric ovens and gas ovens are on page 142 (electric is generally more eco-friendly than gas). Put a lid on saucepans when steaming or cooking to speed up the cooking time and to reduce the amount of heat used. There is no need to buy new cooking equipment – use whatever you have at home first, and if you do need something new, buy second-hand if you can.

11. **Buy better bread.** Bread is one of the foods that we waste the most (milk and salad leaves are the others). Get into the habit of freezing bread and taking out what you need each day. Sourdough, rye and wholegrain might seem more expensive, but can be better value as they are more filling. Slice after buying and freeze until needed.

12. **Shop online.** This can remove the temptation to buy things you don't need and be good value as you can plan ahead. We tend to spend more when in a last-minute, starving rush to buy lunch.

Packing your lunch

If you are taking your lunch to work, you are going to need a lunch box, a hot food/soup flask for cold days, and some forks and spoons. The most eco-friendly thing to do is reuse your existing containers until they fall apart. An old school lunch box, something from a second-hand store, a vintage tin, jam jar, Kilner/Mason jar … they can all work. If you like, line an old container with paper or a beeswax wrap before adding your lunch. Use small glass jars for things like dressings, seeds, nuts and soup toppers.

If you need to buy a new box (and a shiny new lunch box can make taking your own lunch to work extra tempting!) look for boxes made from recycled plastic or plant fibres. Boxes with compartments (like bento

boxes) are great, as you can separate bread, crackers, croutons, dried fruit or anything else you want, and they won't go soft or soggy from being in contact with the rest of your lunch.

Aluminium foil and non-plastic clingfilm can be reused a few times, but I like to use beeswax wrap for bagels, wraps and sandwiches – rinse it with warm, soapy water after use, and smooth it out before using again. If your wax wraps start to look crinkled, place them under a cloth and gently iron.

A hot food/soup flask is worth investing in. Check reviews for one that really works and you will get years of good use from it. They are so useful for taking soups, stews, chillis and curries to work. The mark-up on hot food is far greater than cold, and you can recoup the cost of a hot food flask in just days. Heat the flask before adding your lunch by rinsing it with boiling water – this helps to keep the food hot until lunchtime.

A cool bag and ice pack are great for summer, and mean you don't have to rely on a crowded work fridge.

Your usual forks and spoons are just fine – you don't need to go out and buy new plastic or bamboo items, and they are much easier to eat from than those little wooden forks supermarkets hand out.

We all know that buying bottled water and other packaged drinks isn't great for the planet. Neither is going out to buy a new water bottle when you already have three in the cupboard! If you want extra flavour in your water, add slices of cucumber, orange, lemon and lime, or a few raspberries, blueberries or strawberries. A take-out cup for hot drinks will save you a fortune (some coffee stores provide a discount if you bring your own) and you won't be adding to the mountain of single-use drink cups and plastic lids.

Salads

Gorgeous Greek salad

FF 5

Little plastic pots of salad aren't great for the planet, and can be a bit mean on ingredients. Get into the habit of making your own and you won't look back. All the ingredients for this refreshing salad last for ages, so you can shop at the weekend and make this towards the end of the week.

Makes 2 lunches
Prep 5 minutes, plus
30 minutes soaking (optional)

½ **small red onion, peeled and thinly sliced**

3 **tbsp red wine vinegar or balsamic vinegar**

1 **very ripe, large beef tomato, cut into chunks**

½ **small cucumber, cut into chunks**

handful of Kalamata olives, drained

100g (4oz) **feta or feta-style vegan cheese**

1 **tsp dried oregano**

extra-virgin olive oil, for drizzling

sea salt and black pepper

Put the onion in a bowl and pour over the vinegar. Leave to soak for about 30 minutes, if you have time (if you don't, don't worry, the onion will just be a bit stronger).

Put the tomato, cucumber and olives in your lunch boxes or bowls. Mix them together, adding plenty of salt and pepper.

Sprinkle over the onions (with the vinegar) and mix. Place the feta on top (you can break it up if you like), sprinkle over the oregano and drizzle over a little olive oil.

This salad is best eaten at room temperature rather than fridge-cold, so take your lunch box out a little while before you want to eat it.

Butter bean and halloumi salad

NB **5**

I ate a lunch like this in one of my favourite cafés and then came up with this version at home. Cooking the beans gives them a little more bite, and you can eat the salad warm or cold, so it's really flexible if you are out and about with work.

Makes 2–3 lunches
Prep 5 minutes
Cooking 5 minutes

1 tbsp extra-virgin rapeseed oil or olive oil

2 spring onions/scallions, roughly chopped

1 red bell pepper, seeded and chopped

1 x 400g (14oz) can cooked butter/lima beans

200g (7oz) halloumi or halloumi-style vegan cheese, cubed

2 tsp dried mixed herbs or oregano

2 tbsp apple cider vinegar or wine vinegar

black pepper

2 handfuls of salad leaves

Heat the oil in a large frying pan or skillet over a medium heat and add the spring onions, red pepper, butter beans and halloumi. Cook for 5 minutes, stirring often, until the butter beans have taken on a little colour and the halloumi is slightly browned.

Add the herbs and vinegar, then stir and season to taste with black pepper. Serve on top of the salad leaves. Toss just before eating so the leaves are coated in some of the oil and vinegar.

— Dried vs cooked?

Is it more eco to cook beans and pulses from scratch, or to buy them precooked in cans and jars? It is cheaper to buy dried, and if you buy from a refill store, you cut back on packaging. But you do need to factor in cooking costs and time, and using ready-cooked is quicker and easier. The most eco thing to do is eat less meat, so as long as you eat more pulses and beans, it probably doesn't matter too much how you buy them.

Roasted purple-sprouting broccoli and carrots with black lentils and chipotle

(FF) (LL) (W)

Broccoli and carrots take on new flavours when roasted, so this is an easy way to make everyday vegetables a bit more interesting. Prep some extras if you are cooking on a Sunday, and that means Monday lunch is sorted. Chipotle paste is a quick way to add flavour; keep a jar in the fridge for when you need it.

Makes 1 lunch
Prep 5 minutes
Cooking 20 minutes

½ tsp chipotle chilli paste

2 tsp extra-virgin rapeseed oil or olive oil

handful of purple sprouting broccoli (about 3 stems)

2 carrots, peeled and cut on the diagonal into 1cm (½in) slices

2 tbsp cooked black or green lentils

½ red bell pepper, seeded and thinly sliced

handful of watercress

zest and juice of ½ lemon

sea salt and black pepper

Preheat the oven to 220°C/475°F (if it's not already on for something else).

Mix together the chipotle chilli paste and oil. Put the broccoli and carrots in a small roasting tray and stir in the chipotle oil. Roast for 20 minutes, then remove from the oven and leave to cool.

Put the lentils, red pepper, watercress and the roasted broccoli and carrots in your lunch box or a bowl. Add the lemon zest and juice, stir and season to taste.

— Fridge forage
Haven't got one of the ingredients? It doesn't matter! Swap the carrots for chunks of sweet potato, butternut squash or sweetcorn. Or use a few radishes, sugar snap peas or petits pois instead of the red bell pepper. Use rocket/arugula instead of watercress.

Broad bean, petits pois and green bean salad with hazelnuts and clementine dressing

We get broad/fava beans in our veg box for a few weeks each summer, and this quick salad shows their lime-green beauty at its best. Eat this salad with a piece of baguette or sourdough. The juice of a clementine, satsuma or any other orange mixed with some oil makes a delicious, easy dressing.

Makes 1 lunch
Prep 10 minutes
Cooking 3 minutes

large handful of fresh
  broad/fava beans,
  podded

2 tbsp frozen petits pois

handful of green beans, cut
  in half

25g (1oz) hazelnuts

handful of watercress

zest and juice of
  1 clementine or satsuma

1 tbsp extra-virgin rapeseed
  oil or olive oil

sea salt and black pepper

Cook the broad beans, petits pois and green beans in a pan of simmering water for 3 minutes, then drain in a colander and rinse under cold running water.

Meanwhile, roughly chop the hazelnuts (or bash them with a rolling pin if easier) until you have small pieces.

Peel the broad beans and discard the skins.

Put all the beans and peas in your lunch box or a bowl. Add the watercress and hazelnuts and mix well.

Mix the clementine or satsuma zest and juice with the oil, adding plenty of salt and pepper. Pour the dressing over the salad.

Salads

Sesame noodles with broccoli, sugar snap peas and cashews

5 **LL**

Surprisingly quick to make (I promise!), this noodle lunch is packed with protein and flavour. It's great if you're working at home, or make it in the morning to take to work. If you like your lunch extra spicy, feel free to add more tamari and chilli flakes.

Makes 1 lunch
Prep 5 minutes
Cooking 5 minutes

50g (2oz) soba or buckwheat noodles

2–3 broccoli florets, cut into bite-size pieces

handful of frozen edamame beans

8 sugar snap peas, roughly chopped

2 tbsp sesame or extra-virgin rapeseed oil

1 tbsp tamari or soy sauce

1cm (½in) piece of fresh ginger, peeled and grated

¼ tsp chilli flakes

25g (1oz) cashews

2 tsp sesame seeds

handful of fresh coriander/cilantro, chopped

lime wedge, to serve

Bring a large saucepan of water to a boil. Add the noodles, broccoli, edamame beans and sugar snap peas and cook for 5 minutes. Tip everything into a colander and rinse under cold running water for a few seconds to cool.

Meanwhile, put the oil, tamari or soy sauce, ginger and chilli flakes in a bowl and stir. Chop the cashews until you have small pieces.

Put the noodles and vegetables in your lunch box or a bowl, add the sauce and stir. Sprinkle over the cashews, sesame seeds and coriander and mix. Squeeze over the lime when you're ready to eat.

Smashed beetroot rainbow salad with hazelnut dukkah

FF **LL**

Beetroot/beet looks so vibrant that you know it is going to be good for you. We seem to get it in our veg box quite a lot, so we had to learn how to cook it! Use the leftover leaves in a stir fry (just like rainbow chard or bok choy). You can also buy cooked beetroot in glass jars but you might want to rinse off the pickling vinegar before use. (Avoid using vacuum-packed beetroot, as the packaging adds to the mountain of plastic waste.)

Makes 2 lunches
Prep 10 minutes
Cooking 2 hours (if cooking your beetroots from scratch)

2 medium beetroots/beets, raw or cooked

1 tbsp tahini

squeeze of lemon juice (optional)

For the dukkah

25g (1oz) hazelnuts

50g (2oz) almonds

1 tsp black or white sesame seeds

1 tsp dried mixed herbs

For the rainbow salad

1 carrot, cut into ribbons

2 handfuls of watercress or rocket/arugula

1 courgette/zucchini, grated or spiralized

5–6 radishes, sliced

5–6 cherry or small tomatoes, cut in half

If using raw beetroot, wash well, snip off the stems and leaves, then wrap in foil. Roast for 2 hours at about 200°C/425°F (ideally when the oven is on for something else), then remove and set aside. When cool, peel and chop into rough chunks.

To make the smash, put the cooked beetroot, tahini and lemon juice (if using) in a blender and whizz until smashed but not too smooth. If you don't have a blender, just chop the beetroot finely, and mix it in a bowl with the tahini and lemon.

To make the dukkah, put the hazelnuts and almonds in a blender and whizz until you have small pieces, or just roughly chop them with a knife or smash in a mortar and pestle. Mix them with the seeds and herbs.

Arrange the rainbow salad veggies in two lunch boxes or bowls. Add the beetroot smash. Just before eating, sprinkle over the dukkah.

— Eat the rainbow

Eating veggies the colours of the rainbow is an easy way to get a range of nutrients into your day. Swap in whatever you like to get a different salad every time, such as red cabbage, radicchio, roasted red onion, orange bell pepper, sweetcorn, yellow beetroots/beets, edamame beans, peas, sugar snap peas, broccoli or asparagus.

Salads

Burrito box with charred sweetcorn and avocado and lime salsa

5 **LL**

Charring fresh corn gives it a caramelized, smoky flavour, but if you are in a rush, you can use precooked canned kernels and then this lunch is even quicker. Eat this burrito box on its own or with tortilla chips (see below). If you have thick yoghurt in the fridge, why not add a dollop?

Makes 2 lunches
Prep 5 minutes
Cooking 5 minutes

1 corn on the cob

1 ripe avocado

10 ripe vine or cherry tomatoes, cut in half

¼ red bell pepper, seeded and roughly chopped

zest and juice of 1 lime

¼ tsp chilli flakes (or ¼ fresh chilli, finely chopped)

4 tbsp cooked beans (red haricot, navy, kidney or black)

sea salt and black pepper

Heat a frying pan or skillet over a medium heat. Strip the kernels from the cob using a sharp knife. Put the corn kernels in the pan and cook for 5 minutes until they are charred at the edges.

Meanwhile, cut the avocado in half, remove the stone and scoop out the flesh using a teaspoon so you have rough chunks. Put the avocado, tomatoes and red pepper in a bowl and add half of the lime zest and juice. Add the chilli and plenty of sea salt and stir.

Put the beans in a bowl and add the rest of the lime zest and juice. Add a little salt and black pepper and mix well.

Divide the beans, charred corn and salsa between your two lunch boxes.

— Baked tortilla chips
If you have a spare tortilla wrap, or one that is slightly past its best, snip it into triangles using scissors. Put the triangles on a baking sheet, drizzle over a little oil and bake in a hot oven (ideally, when it is being used for something else) for about 8 minutes, until crisp at the edges.

Black lentil and red pepper salad with blitzed olives

5 **LL** **FF**

Glass jars of olives and cans of lentils are so useful to have in the cupboard, ready for lunch. Add bell peppers and rocket/arugula, which last for ages in the fridge, and lunch is ready! The blitzed olives and lemon make this a flavour-packed meal.

Makes 1 lunch
Prep 5 minutes

handful of rocket/arugula

⅓ red bell pepper, cut into pieces

50g (2oz) cooked Puy or beluga lentils

1 spring onion/scallion, roughly sliced

zest and juice of ½ lemon

25g (1oz) pitted Kalamata olives, drained

1 tsp extra-virgin rapeseed oil or olive oil

black pepper

Put the rocket in your lunch box or a bowl. Add the red pepper, lentils and spring onion and stir. Add the lemon zest and season with pepper.

Put the olives, lemon juice and oil in a blender and whizz until smooth.

Spoon the olive dressing over the salad just before eating.

— Fridge forage
I make a variation of this salad most weeks. To mix it up a little, add whatever veggies you have in the fridge – radishes, sugar snap peas, cherry tomatoes and grated carrot all go well in this. You could also add soft or crumbly cheese.

Protein-packed Buddha bowl with tahini dressing

(LL) (FF)

Buddha bowls are a mix of grains, proteins and vegetables (hot or cold) and they make a colourful, balanced lunch. They are also a great way to use up leftovers. Quinoa is widely available now, so you might be able to buy it grown locally to you; great for low food miles. It is a complete protein, so a really useful grain to have in the cupboard. Some stores sell fresh tofu, which helps with reducing packaging, as most imported tofu comes in plastic.

Makes 2 lunches
Prep 5 minutes
Cooking 20 minutes

1 sweet potato, peeled and cubed

200g (7oz) cooked carlin peas or chickpeas, drained

100g (4oz) firm smoked tofu, cubed

1 tbsp extra-virgin rapeseed oil or olive oil

1 tsp smoked paprika

75g (3oz) quinoa (a mix of red, white and black is nice)

handful of spinach leaves

2 spring onions/scallions, chopped

1 tsp black or white sesame seeds

1 lime, cut in half

sea salt and black pepper

For the tahini dressing
1 tbsp tahini
1 tbsp yoghurt (natural or soya)

Preheat the oven to 200°C/425°F (if it's not already on for something else).

Put the sweet potato, carlin peas or chickpeas and tofu in a baking tray. Mix the oil and paprika and drizzle the mixture over the contents of the tray. Mix well. Roast for 20 minutes, until everything is crispy at the edges. Remove from the oven and leave to cool.

Meanwhile, cook the quinoa for 20 minutes in a pan of simmering water. When cooked, drain and leave to cool.

Now make the dressing: put the tahini and yoghurt in a bowl and mix together. Add a little tap water and mix again until the dressing has a smooth pouring consistency. Season to taste with salt and pepper.

Arrange the spinach leaves and spring onions in two bowls or lunch boxes, then add the roasted sweet potato, carlin peas or chickpeas and tofu, followed by the quinoa. Sprinkle with sesame seeds. Squeeze over the lime and drizzle over the dressing just before eating.

— Carlin peas
You can use carlin peas in the same way as chickpeas; they have a delicious nutty flavour and can be used in hotpots, stews, curries and salads. They have been grown in the UK and northern Europe for many years and you might know them as brown or 'badger' peas.

Monday leftovers lunch

W **LL**

This 'recipe' is more of a prompt to use your roast dinner leftovers. If you don't tend to have many leftovers, get into the habit of roasting a few extras to make lunch the next day. Roasted red onions, parsnips and potatoes make a great base for a salad – you can also chuck in any leftover cooked carrots, green beans and broccoli too.

Makes 2 lunches
Prep 5 minutes
Cooking 20–25 minutes

25g (1oz) quinoa

large handful of rocket/
    arugula or watercress

a few leftover cooked
    carrots, broccoli florets,
    sprouts or other veg

zest and juice of ½ lemon

1 tbsp pumpkin seeds or
    pine nuts

For the roast vegetables

1 sweet potato, cut into
    small wedges (no need
    to peel)

1 red onion, peeled and
    cut into small wedges

1 parsnip, peeled and
    cut into wedges

2 garlic cloves (no need
    to peel)

handful of cherry or
    vine tomatoes

2 tbsp extra-virgin rapeseed
    oil or olive oil

sea salt and black pepper

Preheat the oven to 200°C/425°C (if it's not already on for something else).

Put the sweet potato, onion, parsnip, garlic and tomatoes in a large baking tray. Drizzle over the oil, season with plenty of salt and pepper and roast the vegetables for 20 minutes. When cooked, remove from the oven and leave to cool. The sweet potato wedges might need an extra 5 minutes, depending on their size. Squeeze the garlic out of its skin and chop the flesh.

Meanwhile, cook the quinoa for 20 minutes in a pan of simmering water. When cooked, drain and leave to cool.

When ready to prep your salad, put the rocket or watercress in your lunch boxes or bowls. Add the roast vegetables, quinoa, garlic and any leftover cooked vegetables, and the lemon zest and juice. Sprinkle over the pumpkin seeds or pine nuts and mix gently.

— Mix up your roast veg

Many vegetables roast really well, and make great bases for salads. Here are a few more to try: radishes, beetroot/beet, bell peppers, Brussels sprouts and butternut squash.

Sesame halloumi with quinoa and pomegranate

NB

If you have a Middle Eastern store nearby, you can pick up fresh herbs and pomegranates with minimal plastic packaging. Choose a really ripe pomegranate and you can just squeeze out the seeds and juice over this lunch; there is no need to buy packs of pre-popped seeds. This lunch is nice hot or cold, so you can take it work, or eat it at home.

Makes 2 lunches
Prep 5 minutes
Cooking 20 minutes

50g (2oz) quinoa, rinsed

225g (8oz) halloumi or halloumi-style vegan cheese, sliced

2 tsp runny honey or pomegranate molasses

1 tsp black sesame seeds

handful of fresh parsley, chopped

handful of fresh mint, chopped

about 10 pitted Kalamata or green olives, cut in half

1 ripe pomegranate

black pepper

Preheat the oven to 200°C/425°F (if it's not already on for something else).

Cook the quinoa for 20 minutes in a pan of simmering water. When cooked, drain and leave to cool.

Meanwhile, place the halloumi on a non-stick baking sheet. Spoon over the honey or pomegranate molasses and sprinkle over the sesame seeds. Bake in the oven for 10 minutes until slightly browned.

Put the cooked quinoa in your lunch boxes or bowls. Add the parsley, mint, olives and a little black pepper and mix.

Place the baked halloumi on top. Cut the pomegranate in half and squeeze over the salad so that the juice and seeds fall onto it.

Salads

Roasted cauliflower, carlin pea and grape salad

NB **LL**

Grapes are delicious roasted, and if you have some slightly past their best, this is a great way to use them up. If you roast the cauliflower, carlins and grapes the night before, you can put the rest of this salad together in moments before work.

Makes 2 lunches
Prep 5 minutes
Cooking 20 minutes

1 small cauliflower, cut into small florets

1 x 400g (14oz) can cooked carlin peas or chickpeas, drained and rinsed

2 tbsp extra-virgin rapeseed oil or olive oil

2 handfuls of black or purple seedless grapes

1 tbsp red wine vinegar

handful of watercress or rocket/arugula

100g (4oz) crumbly white cheese (dairy or vegan)

sea salt and black pepper

Preheat the oven to 200°C/425°C (if it's not already on for something else).

Place the cauliflower and carlin peas or chickpeas in a roasting tray and drizzle over about 1 tablespoon of the oil. Mix to coat, then add the grapes. Roast for 20 minutes. Remove from the oven and leave to cool.

Combine the remaining oil with the red wine vinegar. Season with plenty of salt and pepper.

Arrange the watercress or rocket leaves in your lunch boxes or bowls. Tip in the roasted ingredients and crumble over the cheese. Add the dressing when you're ready to eat.

Simple slaws and spirals

LL **5**

Store-bought slaws often come in plastic pots, so here are some easy ways to make your own. Slaws are great in bagels, sourdough sandwiches and wraps, or you can have some alongside your chilli, curry or stew. Making slaw is a really easy way to get more vegetables into your lunch and it's also great for using up any lonely veggies in the bottom of the fridge. Each slaw will keep for 1–2 days in the fridge.

Makes 2–4 sides
Prep 5 minutes

¼ **small white or red cabbage, thinly sliced**

1 **raw beetroot/beet, grated (no need to peel)**

1 **carrot, peeled and grated**

3 **radishes, thinly sliced**

1 **tbsp apple cider vinegar**

1 **tbsp extra-virgin rapeseed oil or olive oil**

2 **tbsp pumpkin seeds or peanuts**

sea salt and black pepper

RED SUMMER SLAW WITH RADISHES

Put the cabbage, beetroot, carrot and radishes in a bowl and mix well.

Mix the vinegar and oil in a bowl and season with plenty of salt and pepper. Pour this dressing over the slaw and mix well. Sprinkle over the pumpkin seeds or peanuts.

Makes 4 sides
Prep 10 minutes

¼ **small red cabbage, thinly sliced**

½ **small red onion, peeled and sliced, or 4 spring onions/scallions, sliced**

1 **carrot, peeled and grated**

2 **tbsp thick yoghurt (Greek, soya or natural)**

1 **tsp wholegrain mustard**

1 **tbsp apple cider vinegar**

sea salt and black pepper

RAINBOW COLESLAW

Put the cabbage, onion and carrot in a bowl and mix well.

Mix the yoghurt, mustard and vinegar in a bowl and season with plenty of salt and pepper. Pour the dressing over the slaw and mix well.

Makes 2 sides
Prep 5 minutes

1 courgette/zucchini,
   green or yellow

1 carrot, peeled

1 eating apple (no need
   to peel)

zest and juice of ½ lime

1 tbsp extra-virgin rapeseed
   oil or olive oil

sea salt and black pepper

COURGETTE, CARROT, APPLE AND LIME SLAW

Spiralize or grate the courgette and carrot into a bowl. Grate the apple and add it to the bowl.

Mix the lime zest and juice with the oil and season with plenty of salt and pepper. Add to the bowl and mix well.

— More things to put in slaws

Celeriac, peas, green beans, sugar snap peas, sweetcorn, dried fruits, fresh herbs, seeds, nuts … whatever you like!

Salads

Hassle-free salad dressings

5 NB LL

No more buying those mini plastic pots of salad dressings! It's really easy to make your own, so there's no need to add to the plastic mountains to add flavour to your lunch. You probably already have ingredients you can use in your cupboards, fridge and fruit bowl – here is a list of ingredients you can experiment with, following this simple method:

Oil (2–3 tsp) + Acid (1 tsp) + Extras (to taste) = Dressing

<u>OIL</u> +	<u>ACID</u> +	<u>EXTRAS</u>
— Extra-virgin rapeseed oil	— Apple cider vinegar	— Mustard
— Extra-virgin olive oil	— Balsamic vinegar	— Honey
— Sesame oil	— Red or white wine vinegar	— Sea salt
— Walnut oil	— Lemon juice	— Black pepper
	— Lime juice	— Dried herbs
	— Orange juice	— Fresh herbs
	— Pomegranate juice	— Fresh ginger
		— Harissa paste
		— Pesto
		— Tamari sauce
		— Soy sauce
		— Tahini

Serves 1

1 tbsp apple cider vinegar

2 tbsp extra-virgin
  rapeseed oil

sea salt and black pepper,
  to taste

FLEXI VINAIGRETTE

A basic, everyday dressing that you can use for
any salad. You can double it up, swap in other oils
and acids, add extra flavours – have a go!

Put everything in a small bowl and whisk together
with a fork.

1 tbsp yoghurt
  (Greek-style or soya)

½ tsp harissa paste

HARISSA YOGHURT DRESSING

Spoon this one over roast vegetable salads.

Put the yoghurt and harissa paste in a small bowl and mix
together. Add a little water if you want a thinner dressing.

2 tbsp extra-virgin
  rapeseed oil

zest and juice of ½ lime

5mm (¼in) piece of fresh
  ginger, peeled and
  grated

a few sprigs of fresh mint,
  finely chopped

sea salt and black pepper,
  to taste

LIME, GINGER AND MINT DRESSING

Zingy and delicious, this goes well on so many green
leafy salads and slaws. Swap the lime for satsuma or
lemon another day.

Put everything in a small bowl and whisk together
with a fork.

— Packing tip

If you are taking your lunch to work, take your dressing
in a mini jam jar and add it just before eating so the salad
stays crisp.

Salads

Hot

Puy lentil, tomato and cannellini bean pot with harissa

W **NB**

Lentils and beans are so useful to have in the cupboard, ready to make warming stews. Eat this hotpot with a slaw and/or flatbread, or just as it is. Harissa paste is an easy way to add flavour – it's made with chillies and spices. A little jar more than earns its place in the kitchen.

Makes 3 lunches
Prep 5 minutes
Cooking 25 minutes

1 tbsp extra-virgin rapeseed oil or olive oil

1 small onion, peeled and chopped

1 carrot, peeled and chopped

1 garlic clove, peeled and chopped

1 x 400g (14oz) can cooked Puy or beluga lentils, drained

1 x 400g (14oz) can chopped tomatoes

1 x 400g (14oz) cooked cannellini beans, drained and rinsed

1 tbsp harissa paste

sea salt and black pepper

lime wedges, to serve

Put the oil, onion, carrot and garlic in a large saucepan and cook over a gentle heat for 10 minutes, until the onion has softened.

Add the lentils, tomatoes and cannellini beans and stir well. Add about 3 tablespoons of tap water and cook over a gentle heat with the lid off for 15 minutes, until the liquid has reduced.

Stir in the harissa paste, cook for another minute, then taste and season with salt and pepper. Serve with lime wedges to squeeze over just before eating. Extra portions can be frozen for another day.

Chickpea, apricot and almond hotpot

If you have a refill store near you, you can buy most of the ingredients you'll need for this recipe – spices, dried fruit and ground almonds are sold loose, so you can buy just what you need. Save up glass jars of all sizes to take with you. Eat this hotpot with naan, rice or a slaw (see pages 40–1).

Makes 4 lunches
Prep 5 minutes
Cooking 15 minutes

1 tbsp extra-virgin rapeseed oil

1 onion, peeled and chopped

1 garlic clove, peeled and finely chopped

1cm (½in) piece of fresh ginger, peeled and finely chopped

2 tsp cumin seeds

1 tsp ground turmeric

½ tsp chilli flakes

1 tbsp garam masala

1 x 400g (14oz) can chickpeas or carlin peas, drained and rinsed

1 x 400g (14oz) can chopped tomatoes

6 dried or fresh apricots, chopped

2 tbsp ground almonds

Heat the oil in a medium saucepan over a low heat and add the onion, garlic, ginger and cumin seeds. Cover and cook for 10 minutes, until the onion has softened.

Add the turmeric, chilli flakes and garam masala and stir, then add the chickpeas, chopped tomatoes, apricots and ground almonds. Stir and cook for 5 minutes, with the lid off, until the sauce has thickened a little.

— Zero food waste
You can also add spare vegetables to this curry, such as a few green beans, spinach leaves or chard.

Hot

Black lentil, almond and coconut dhal with crispy cauliflower

(W) (NB)

This creamy, mild dhal is packed with protein from the lentils, almonds and yoghurt, so you should have plenty of energy for a busy afternoon. Once you've chopped a few things, it's not a lot of work; double it up to make extra for more lunches. Eat with a naan bread or slaw (see pages 40–1).

Makes 2 lunches
Prep 5 minutes
Cooking 35 minutes

extra-virgin rapeseed oil, for frying and roasting

1 small red onion, peeled and finely chopped

1 garlic clove, peeled and chopped

1cm (½in) piece of fresh ginger, peeled and grated

1 fresh red chilli, seeded and chopped

1 x 400g (14oz) can black beluga lentils, drained and rinsed

3 tsp garam masala

200g (7oz) chopped tomatoes or passata

1 tbsp ground almonds

1 small cauliflower, cut into very small florets

2 tbsp coconut yoghurt

sea salt

Heat a little oil in a large saucepan over a low heat, add the onion and cook for at least 10 minutes, until softened. Add the garlic, ginger and chilli and cook for 5 minutes.

Preheat the oven to 200°C/425°C (if it's not already on for something else).

Add the lentils, 2 teaspoons of the garam masala, the tomatoes and almonds to the pan, then add 100ml (4fl oz/½ cup) water, stir well, pop on the lid and bring to a gentle simmer. Cook for 20 minutes.

Meanwhile, put the cauliflower florets (and any small leaves) in a large roasting tray, drizzle over some oil, and sprinkle over the remaining garam masala. Roast for 15 minutes until the florets are charred at the edges.

Remove the dhal from the heat and stir through the coconut yoghurt. Season to taste with salt.

If you're taking it to work, put your dhal in a food flask and the cauliflower in a separate pot. Reheat the dhal if you need to, and place the cauliflower on top of it.

— Love your leftovers
Roasted cauliflower is great to have in the fridge to add to salads throughout the week. Roast any smaller leaves when you roast the florets; these are nice to eat as well.

Hot

Red bean and sweetcorn chilli with lime and coriander drizzle

(W)

If you always make chilli with kidney beans, why not try a bean grown closer to home? Red haricot, pinto and adzuki beans are all great in chilli, and you might be able to cut down on your food miles. This is a very quick, low-effort chilli that you can knock up if eating lunch at home today, or you can prep ahead and keep in the fridge for up to 3 days, or put in the freezer for a later date (make the drizzle on the day you want to eat it). Serve with cornbread, flatbread or Baked tortilla chips (see page 16).

Makes 3 lunches
Prep 5 minutes
Cooking 20 minutes

2 tbsp extra-virgin
    rapeseed oil

1 red onion, peeled
    and chopped

1 garlic clove, peeled
    and chopped

1 red or orange bell pepper,
    seeded and chopped

1 tsp hot chilli powder or
    chilli flakes, plus extra
    to taste

1 tsp ground cumin

100g (4oz) sweetcorn
    kernels, fresh, frozen
    or canned and drained

1 x 400g (14oz) can red
    haricot or kidney beans,
    drained and rinsed

1 x 400g (14oz) can
    chopped tomatoes

1 carrot, peeled and chopped

sea salt and black pepper

For the lime and coriander drizzle

zest and juice of 1 lime

handful of fresh coriander/
    cilantro, chopped (or
    2 tbsp frozen, chopped)

Heat the oil in a large saucepan over a low heat, then add the onion, garlic and pepper. Cook for 10 minutes, until the onion has softened.

Add the chilli powder or flakes and cumin, and stir through the onion mixture.

Add the sweetcorn, red beans, tomatoes and carrot, and stir. Bring to a simmer and cook for 10 minutes with the lid off until any liquid has reduced and the chilli has thickened. Season to taste with salt and pepper and a little extra chilli if you like.

Whizz the lime zest, juice and coriander in a blender. Pour over the chilli when you're ready to eat.

— Love your leftovers
If you have any leftover fresh coriander/cilantro, you can freeze it and use it another time to make a drizzle or stir into curries and chillis for extra flavour. It loses its structure but will be just fine for cooking and drizzles.

Hot

Easy aubergine caponata with capers, olives and pine nuts

W **NB**

It can take hours to make a traditional Sicilian caponata, but this one is quick and, thanks to the capers and olives, it's still full of flavour. I like it piled onto hot sourdough toast or with focaccia. It will keep in the fridge for about 3 days.

Makes 2–3 lunches
Prep 5 minutes
Cooking 30 minutes

2 tbsp extra-virgin
    rapeseed oil
1 small aubergine/eggplant
    (about 225g/8oz), cut
    into chunks
1 small red onion, peeled
    and chopped
1 garlic clove, peeled and
    chopped
1 x 400g (14oz) can
    chopped tomatoes
2 tsp capers, drained
50g (2oz) pitted Kalamata
    or green olives
1 tsp red wine vinegar
    (optional)
2 tbsp pine nuts
sea salt and black pepper

Heat the oil in a large saucepan over a low heat. Add the aubergine, onion and garlic, put the lid on, and cook for 10 minutes until the onion is softened.

Add the tomatoes, capers and olives. Bring to a simmer and cook for 20 minutes with the lid off until the liquid has reduced.

Stir in the red wine vinegar, if using, and season to taste, then stir in the pine nuts.

Hot

Winter veg box bake with tahini yoghurt dressing

W NB LL

Roast vegetables at the weekend and you will have a base that you can use to make a few lunches during the week. You can then vary your lunch by adding fresh leaves, walnuts, chickpeas, butter/lima beans … whatever you like. Swede, celeriac and potatoes would also work well; just use them instead of the butternut squash or parsnips. It's lovely hot or cold.

Makes 3–4 lunches
Prep 10 minutes
Cooking 30 minutes

2 red onions, peeled and cut into wedges

1 butternut squash, seeded and cut into chunks (peeled or not, up to you)

2 carrots, peeled and cut into chunks

2 parsnips, peeled and cut into chunks

2 tbsp extra-virgin rapeseed oil or olive oil

1 tbsp smoked paprika

1 tbsp pine nuts (optional)

For the tahini yoghurt dressing

1 tbsp tahini

2 tbsp natural-style yoghurt

juice of ½ lemon

sea salt and black pepper

Preheat the oven to 220°C/475°C (if it's not already on for something else).

Put the onions, squash, carrots and parsnips in a large roasting tray and spread them out into a single layer. Mix the oil with the paprika and drizzle it over the vegetables. Stir to coat, then roast in the oven for 30 minutes, giving everything a stir about halfway through.

Meanwhile, put the tahini, yoghurt and lemon juice in a bowl and mix together. Add a little tap water and stir until the mixture has a smooth pouring consistency. Season with salt and pepper.

When ready to eat, pour over the tahini yoghurt dressing and sprinkle over the pine nuts, if using.

— Squash seeds

If you like, roast the squash seeds alongside the vegetables, and sprinkle them over instead of pine nuts. Not all squash seeds roast very well; it depends on the variety, but why not give it a go before throwing them away? Just drizzle a little oil over them and roast for about 20 minutes alongside the vegetables.

Hot

Summer veg box bake with lemon and pumpkin seeds

(W) (NB) (LL)

If you have a surfeit of courgettes/zucchini or other summer veg, use them up in this easy one-tray bake. You can then mix and match with other ingredients to make lunches during the week. Summer squashes, carrots, radishes, beetroot/beet and corn all roast well too, so you can use up all your spare vegetables! Leftover beans, rice or couscous go great with this, or use it to fill a chunk of ciabatta.

Makes 3 lunches
Prep 10 minutes
Cooking 25 minutes

2 red onions, peeled and
    cut into small wedges

2 courgettes/zucchini,
    roughly sliced

1 red bell pepper, seeded
    and cut into chunks

200g (7oz) cherry or other
    small tomatoes

100g (4oz) green beans, cut
    in half

1 tbsp extra-virgin rapeseed
    oil or olive oil

1 garlic clove, peeled
    and roughly chopped

To serve
3 handfuls of rocket/
    arugula

1 tbsp pumpkin seeds

zest and juice of 1 lemon

Preheat the oven to 220°C/475°C (if it's not already on for something else).

Put the onions, courgettes, pepper, tomatoes and green beans in a large roasting tray and spread them out into a single layer (you might need two trays). Drizzle over the oil, add the garlic and stir to coat all the vegetables. Roast for 25 minutes, giving everything a stir about halfway through.

Mix the veg with a handful of rocket per serving. Sprinkle over some pumpkin seeds and add the lemon zest and juice. You could also stir in any leftover cooked pulses and grains you might have to hand. Eat warm or cold.

Hot

Jackfruit and green bean curry

Cans of jackfruit are now pretty easy to find, so if you are bored with your usual hot lunches, try this recipe for a change. Make a batch, freeze the extra portions, and lunch is sorted for another day. Eat with rice or a naan. Slaw is good with this too (see pages 40–1).

Makes 4 lunches
Prep 5 minutes
Cooking 40 minutes

2 tbsp extra-virgin rapeseed oil or coconut oil

1 red onion, peeled and thinly sliced

2 garlic cloves, peeled and chopped

2cm (¾in) piece of fresh ginger, peeled and grated

½ tsp mustard seeds

1 tbsp garam masala

½ tsp chilli powder or chilli flakes

1 tbsp tomato purée/paste

1 x 565g (20oz) can green/young jackfruit, drained and rinsed

120ml (4fl oz/½ cup) coconut milk

100g (4oz) green beans, cut in half

black pepper

lime wedges, to serve

Heat the oil in a large saucepan over a low heat and add the onion, garlic and ginger. Cook for 10 minutes, until the onion has softened, then add the mustard seeds, garam masala, chilli powder or chilli flakes and tomato purée and stir together. Cook for 1 minute. Add the jackfruit, coconut milk and 150ml (5fl oz/½ cup) water. Bring to a boil, then reduce the heat and simmer with the lid on for 15 minutes.

Remove the lid and shred the jackfruit using two forks. Add the green beans and cook with the lid off for 10 minutes.

Add black pepper to taste (jackfruit in brine can be quite salty, so you probably won't need to add salt). Squeeze over plenty of fresh lime juice just before eating.

— Love your leftovers
You could also add a few chopped spinach leaves or chard to this curry, when you add the beans.

Hot

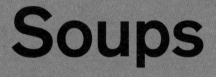

Soups

Tomato, pepper and butter bean soup

W **NB**

Many of the ready-made soups you can buy lack protein, so you can end up feeling hungry later in the day. Butter beans are packed with protein and give soups a lovely creamy texture. If you have leftover bread of any kind, you can turn it into croutons to put on top of your soups (see page 88). Stir through some cashew cream too, if you like (see page 86).

Makes 3–4 lunches
Prep 10 minutes
Cooking 25 minutes

1 tbsp extra-virgin rapeseed oil or olive oil

1 onion, peeled and chopped

1 red bell pepper, seeded and chopped

1 carrot, peeled and chopped

1 garlic clove, peeled and chopped

1 x 400g (14oz) can chopped tomatoes

1 x 400g (14oz) can butter/lima beans, drained and rinsed

sea salt and black pepper

Heat the oil in a large saucepan over a low heat, add the onion, red pepper, carrot and garlic and cook, with the lid on, for 10 minutes until softened.

Add the tomatoes and butter beans and stir. Fill the tomato can with tap water, pour it into the soup mixture and stir again. Bring to a boil, reduce the heat and cook for 15 minutes. Season with salt and pepper.

Blend the soup or leave it chunky – it's up to you. This makes a comforting, thick soup, but you can add a little more water to loosen it if you like.

— An alternative

Grate fresh beetroot/beet into this soup when you add the tomatoes for a vibrant variation.

Soups

Cauliflower and cashew soup with crispy carlins

W **NB** **LL**

Cauliflower makes a really soothing, creamy soup. To be more eco-friendly, roast your cauliflower, onion and carlins when the oven is on for something else, then store in the fridge so this soup is really quick to make when you need it. You can buy cashews and sometimes cashew pieces from refill stores (the pieces are cheaper and save you some chopping work).

Makes 2 lunches
Prep 5 minutes
Cooking 30 minutes

1 small cauliflower, chopped into florets

1 onion, peeled and cut into small wedges

100g (4oz) cooked carlin peas or chickpeas, drained and rinsed

2 tbsp extra-virgin rapeseed oil or olive oil

50g (2oz) unsalted cashews

500ml (17fl oz/2 cups) vegetable stock or water

sea salt and black pepper

1 tsp chilli flakes, to serve

Preheat the oven to 200°C/425°C (if it's not already on for something else).

Put the cauliflower and onion on one side of a large roasting tray and the carlin peas on the other. Drizzle over the oil and roast for 20 minutes.

Meanwhile, chop the cashews as finely as you can, or put them in a blender and whizz until you have small pieces.

Remove the tray from the oven. Spoon the cauliflower and onion into a saucepan, leaving a few small cauliflower florets and the carlin peas behind.

Add the stock or water to the saucepan, bring to a boil, then reduce the heat and cook for 10 minutes until the cauliflower is soft.

Add the cashews, stir well, then blend the mixture until smooth. Taste and season with salt and pepper if needed (this will depend on the flavour of your vegetable stock).

Pour the soup into bowls or into soup flasks. Sprinkle over the extra cauliflower florets, the crispy carlin peas and a few chilli flakes. If you're taking the soup to work, take the toppings in a jam jar to add after reheating.

— Cauliflower 'cheese' soup
Whizz 1 tablespoon of nutritional yeast with the cashews to give this soup a cauliflower cheese flavour. You might want to skip adding the chilli flakes.

Pea, spinach and chilli soup

W **NB**

If you keep a large bag of peas in the freezer, you are never far away from a quick, easy lunch! Frozen peas are packed with nutrients, including vitamin C, protein and folates, and although they come wrapped in plastic at the moment, they are an affordable option for many, with low food waste. A hit of chilli and a squeeze of lemon juice just before serving gives this soup a delicious flavour kick and it's also lovely with a little cashew cream (see page 86) or pesto stirred through.

Makes 2 lunches
Prep 5 minutes
Cooking 20 minutes

2 tbsp extra-virgin rapeseed oil or olive oil

1 small onion, peeled and chopped

1 garlic clove, peeled and chopped

1 tsp chilli flakes, plus extra for sprinkling

250g (9oz) frozen peas

100g (4oz) fresh or frozen spinach, chopped

350ml (12fl oz/1½ cups) vegetable stock or water

sea salt and black pepper

lemon wedge, to serve

Heat the oil in a large saucepan over a low heat, add the onion and garlic and cook for 10 minutes, until the onion is softened.

Add the chilli flakes and stir. Cook for 1 minute.

Add the peas, spinach and stock or water. Bring to a boil, reduce to a simmer and cook for 5 minutes, then remove from the heat and blend until smooth. Season to taste with salt and pepper.

Squeeze over some lemon juice just before eating, and sprinkle with a few extra chilli flakes.

Soups

Spicy black bean soup with dark chocolate

LL **NB**

Yes, this really does have chocolate in it! It adds a lovely depth and richness to the soup, and goes so well with the smoked paprika. It's quite a hearty soup, with the black beans providing plenty of protein, but a few Baked tortilla chips with it would be good too (see page 16).

Makes 3 lunches
Prep 5 minutes
Cooking 25 minutes

1 tbsp extra-virgin rapeseed oil or olive oil

1 red onion, peeled and chopped

1 garlic clove, peeled and chopped

1 celery stalk, finely chopped

1 red bell pepper, seeded and thinly sliced

1 tsp smoked paprika

1 x 400g (14oz) can black beans, drained and rinsed

300g (10oz) tomato passata or 1 x 400g (4oz) can chopped tomatoes, blended

25g (1oz) chocolate (70% cocoa solids)

sea salt and black pepper

lime wedges, to serve

Heat the oil in a large saucepan over a low heat, add the onion, garlic, celery and pepper and cook for 10 minutes with the lid on, until the onion is softened.

Stir in the paprika, black beans, passata and 250ml (8fl oz/1 cup) water. Bring to a boil, then reduce the heat and simmer for 15 minutes. Stir in the chocolate until melted, then remove from the heat and season to taste with salt and pepper.

Serve with lime wedges for squeezing over just before eating.

— Black beans

Also known as turtle beans, black beans are so useful to have in the cupboard. They are a good source of protein and iron, and are great in chillis, stews, stir-fries and wraps. You can also whizz them up in a blender to make a spread for your sandwiches, and use them in baking – black bean brownies are great! Cooking from dried takes a bit of planning ahead if you want to eat them for lunch: soak the dried beans overnight, then cook in fresh water on the hob for about an hour (once cooked you can freeze them). Note: 120g (5 oz) dried black beans makes about 240g (9 oz) cooked beans, which you need for this recipe.

Parsnip and apple soup

There are always plenty of parsnips and apples around during the autumn, making this a really good-value soup. Parsnips go well with aromatic spices; I always have garam masala in the cupboard, as you can add lots of flavour with just one jar. I also like this soup with chopped cobnuts sprinkled over, although their season is very short. Hazelnuts are good too.

Makes 3 lunches
Prep 5 minutes
Cooking 20 minutes

2 tbsp extra-virgin rapeseed oil or olive oil

1 red onion, peeled and cut into chunks

1 celery stalk, chopped

1 garlic clove, peeled and chopped

500g (1lb 2oz) parsnips, peeled and cut into small chunks

1 small Bramley or Granny Smith apple, peeled, cored and cut into small chunks

2 tsp garam masala, plus extra to serve (optional)

500ml (17fl oz/2 cups) water or vegetable stock

sea salt and black pepper

Heat the oil in a large saucepan over a low heat, then add the onion, celery, garlic, parsnips and apple. Cook for 10 minutes, with the lid on, until everything has softened.

Stir in the garam masala, add the water or vegetable stock and stir. Bring to a boil, then reduce to a simmer and cook over a low heat, with the lid on, for 10 minutes.

Blend the soup, season to taste with salt and pepper, and a little more garam masala if you like. If the soup is too thick, add a little boiling water to loosen it.

— Garam masala
This aromatic spice blend adds depth of flavour, warmth and sweetness. The blends vary, but usually contain cumin, coriander, fennel, cinnamon and more. It's really useful to have a small jar to add flavour to soups and curries; it will lose depth of flavour if not used up fairly quickly, so buy small amounts if possible.

Leek, kale, potato and lime soup

Break the habit of buying single-use cartons of soup by making a batch of your own. This creamy soup (made without cream) is lovely with a squeeze of fresh lime juice and some crunchy peanuts sprinkled over just before eating. Extra portions can be frozen for another day.

Makes 4 lunches
Prep 10 minutes
Cooking 25 minutes

2 tbsp extra-virgin rapeseed oil or olive oil

2 leeks, sliced

1 onion, peeled and chopped

1 celery stalk, chopped

350g (11oz) white potatoes, peeled and chopped

100g (4oz) trimmed kale, chopped

500ml (17fl oz/2 cups) water or vegetable stock

50g (2oz) unsalted peanuts

zest of 1 lime, and juice to taste

sea salt and black pepper

Heat the oil in a large saucepan over a low heat. When hot, add the leeks, onion and celery, then put the lid on and cook for 10 minutes, until the onion has softened.

Add the potatoes and kale and pour in the water or vegetable stock. Bring to a boil, reduce to a simmer, put the lid back on, and cook for 15 minutes.

Meanwhile, put the peanuts in a mortar and bash with a pestle until you have small pieces.

Blend the soup until smooth, then season to taste with plenty of salt and pepper.

Add the lime zest and squeeze in a little lime juice. Sprinkle over the crushed peanuts just before eating.

Soups

Red miso and smoked tofu pour-over soup

LL **5**

Pour-over soups are practical for taking to work as you don't add the liquid until lunchtime, making them light to carry and leak-proof. You can get so many different types of noodles: wholegrain, soybean, rice, soba, udon, spelt … just choose very thin noodles so they cook quickly in boiling water. Ideally, choose noodles sold in cardboard boxes, which are easier to recycle than plastic.

Makes 1 lunch
Prep 5 minutes

2 tsp red miso paste

5mm (¼in) piece of fresh ginger, peeled and grated

½ small red chilli, seeded and chopped

50g (2oz) dried, thin wholegrain noodles

3 brown or white mushrooms, thinly sliced

100g (4oz) firm smoked tofu, cut into small cubes

1 tbsp sweetcorn kernels, fresh, frozen or canned and drained

4 green beans, thinly sliced

Put all the ingredients into a soup flask or large, sealable heatproof jar. Break the noodles if necessary to fit them in.

Just before eating, pour over enough boiling water to cover all the ingredients. Stir as well as you can, making sure you dissolve the miso. Replace the lid to keep the heat in and leave for 3–5 minutes. Test the noodles for softness and leave for a little longer if necessary. This will depend on the thickness of your noodles.

— Love your leftovers
You can add pretty much anything to your pour-over soup, so it's great for using up stray veggies in the bottom of the fridge. Broccoli, carrots, shredded cabbage, spring onions/scallions, peas and bell peppers all work well; just chop them up small. Sprinkle over a few nuts and seeds too, if you like.

Butternut squash, ginger and blood orange soup

W **NB**

If you have a beautiful squash to use, this soup is the one to make. I love using blood oranges but their season is short, so if they're not available, use any orange that you like. Hazelnut dukkah (see page 27) sprinkled over just before eating adds crunch and depth of flavour, ideal for a delicious autumn lunch. Extra portions can be frozen for another day (or will be fine in the fridge for up to 3 days).

Makes 3 lunches
Prep 10 minutes
Cooking 25 minutes

2 tbsp extra-virgin rapeseed oil or olive oil

1 onion, peeled and chopped

1 carrot, peeled and chopped

1cm (½in) piece of fresh ginger, peeled and grated

1 butternut squash (about 500g/1lb 2oz), peeled, seeded, and roughly chopped

500ml (17fl oz/2 cups) water or vegetable stock

1 blood orange

sea salt and black pepper

Heat the oil in a large saucepan over a low heat. When hot, add the onion, carrot and ginger and cook, with the lid on, for 10 minutes, until the onion has softened.

Add the butternut squash and water or stock. Bring to a boil, then reduce to a simmer and cook for 15 minutes until the squash is soft.

Blend until smooth. Grate over a little of the orange zest, add all of the juice, and stir while heating through. If you need to, add a little more water. Season to taste with salt and pepper.

— Mixing it up
Saffron, smoked paprika and chilli flakes also work well in butternut squash soup, so you can swap out the ginger for any of these if that's what you have.

Stir-ins and sprinkles

(FF) (5) (LL)

If you have made a batch of soup, you can vary the flavour each time with a stir-in or sprinkle. These are a great way to use up any leftovers around the kitchen: bread, herbs, citrus, yoghurt, nuts, seeds, tapenade, pesto and so forth can all be used, and they add extra nutrients to your lunch too.

Makes enough for 2–3 soups

50g (2oz) herbs, including stems, chopped

25g (1oz) pine nuts

1 tbsp extra-virgin rapeseed oil or olive oil

sea salt and black pepper, to taste

LEFTOVER HERB PESTO

If you have tired-looking herbs, whizz them into a stir-in pesto. Parsley, mint, basil, coriander/cilantro and chives all work well on their own, or try a mix of two or more. If you don't have quite enough herbs, use dark green leaves, such as watercress.

Whizz the ingredients together in a blender. It doesn't matter if the pesto isn't smooth; roughly blended is fine. Scoop it out of the blender, give it a mix, season to taste, and use to stir into your soup. The pesto will keep in a jar in the fridge for up to 2 days.

75g (3oz) cashews

CASHEW CREAM

This creamy, comforting stir-in is a lovely addition to Tomato, pepper and butter bean soup (see page 69) and Pea, spinach and chilli soup (see page 73).

Put the cashews in a small heatproof bowl and pour over just enough boiling water to cover them. Leave to soak for 20 minutes, then whizz the nuts with the soaking water in a blender until smooth. Add a little more water if you need to.

Makes 1–2 soup toppers

1–2 slices of day-old bread,
   e.g. sourdough, granary,
   ciabatta, baguette
extra-virgin rapeseed oil
   or olive oil
Flavourings, such as
   dried herbs, salt and
   pepper, chilli flakes and
   nutritional yeast

CROUTONS

Use up your leftover bread to make crispy croutons to sprinkle on your soups and salads. Prep these when the oven is on for something else (anything medium/high temperature is fine but just check so they don't burn).

Snip the bread into pieces using scissors and place in a baking tray. Drizzle over the oil and sprinkle over any flavourings. Shuffle the bread around until every piece of it is coated, then bake for about 15 minutes, until golden and crispy. Store spare croutons in a sealed container in the fridge for a day or two.

Makes 2–3 soup toppers

5 tbsp (⅓ cup) seeds
   (a mixture of pumpkin,
   sesame and sunflower
   is nice)
1 tsp extra-virgin rapeseed
   oil or olive oil
1 tsp tamari or soy sauce

SEED MIX

Add protein, flavour and crunch to your salads and soups with seeds. Prep these when the oven is on for something else (anything medium/high temperature is fine but just check so they don't burn).

Mix the seeds with the oil and the tamari or soy sauce. Spread them over a baking sheet and bake for about 5 minutes until lightly browned. Leave to cool, then store in a jar, ready to sprinkle over your lunch.

Other things you can add to soup:

— Hazelnut dukkah
(see page 27)

— Nut butter

— Crispy carlin peas
or chickpeas (see
page 70)

— Crumbled cheese

— Yoghurt: soya, coconut,
Greek-style, natural

— Sumac, smoked
paprika, chilli flakes,
garam masala

— Spring onions/scallions,
chopped

— Herbs: parsley,
chives, basil, mint,
coriander/cilantro

Soups

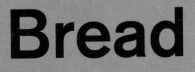

Sandwich fillings

(5) (LL) (NB)

Cheese or hummus? Hummus or cheese? It can be really easy to get into a rut with veggie sandwich fillings, so here are some ideas to help you mix it up a bit. You may find they also help you to cut down on the amount of plastic pots and wrapping in your recycling. Each filling will keep for 1–2 days in the fridge.

Makes 3–4 small pots
Prep 5 minutes

1 x 400g (14oz) can
  chickpeas, drained
  and rinsed
1 garlic clove, peeled
  and chopped, or
  1 tsp garlic powder
2 tbsp extra-virgin rapeseed
  oil or olive oil
zest and juice of ½ lemon
½–1 tsp smoked paprika
sea salt and black pepper

NO-SESAME HUMMUS

Still buying plastic pots of hummus every week? This is an easy switch to cut back on your plastic. Schools and workplaces sometimes have a ban on sesame because of allergies, so here is a no-tahini hummus you can take instead. Use your leftovers (see below) to change the flavour each time you make it.

Put everything in a blender and whizz. Add about 75ml (5 tablespoons) tap water and whizz again to the consistency you prefer. Taste and add salt and pepper and extra paprika, if you like.

— Love your leftovers
Make your hummus different every week by adding some leftover roast onion, roast lemon, fresh or dried coriander/cilantro, fresh or roasted red bell pepper, olives, lime zest and juice, dried sumac, pesto, sun-dried tomatoes…

1 x 400g (14oz) can
  black beans, drained
  and rinsed
1 tsp chipotle paste
zest and juice of 1 lime
sea salt

BLACK BEAN AND LIME MASH

This combination is delicious spread in a tortilla wrap with crunchy salad, or in a lunch box with tortilla chips and strips of pepper and carrot.

Put everything in a blender with 50ml (3 tablespoons) of water. Whizz until mostly smooth, with a few whole beans still intact if you like. Season to taste with salt.

Bread

92

x 400g (14oz) can butter/
lima beans, drained
and rinsed

roasted red bell pepper,
in oil, chopped

½ tsp harissa paste
or smoked paprika

sea salt

BUTTER BEAN AND ROASTED RED PEPPER MASH

This mash is lovely scooped up with warm flatbreads or strips of pitta. Take a few olives, nuts and vegetable sticks in your lunch box too for an easy, snacky lunch.

Put everything in a blender with 50ml (3 tablespoons) of water. Whizz until smooth. Season to taste with salt.

x 400g (14oz) can
chickpeas, drained and
rinsed

tbsp capers, drained

tsp mustard (English,
wholegrain or Dijon)

2 tbsp thick yoghurt (Greek,
natural or soya)

zest and juice of ½ lemon

2 spring onions/scallions,
chopped

2 tbsp cooked sweetcorn
kernels

sea salt and black pepper

CHUNA WITH SWEETCORN

'Chuna' is made with chickpeas, capers and lemon, a veggie alternative to the classic tuna mayo. It is lovely with sweetcorn in crunchy rolls or bagels, or spread on crackers. Jars of capers last for ages in the fridge and are an easy way to get a briny, tangy flavour in sandwiches and pasta sauces.

Put the chickpeas, capers, mustard, yoghurt, lemon zest and juice in a blender. Whizz until roughly blended.

Stir in the spring onions and sweetcorn. Season to taste with salt and pepper.

Bread

Broad bean and pea 'guacamole' on sourdough

NB

If you want to cut down on your avo habit, try this vibrant, protein-packed lunch instead. It's also nice with crumbly cheese on top. If you are taking this to work, just add another slice and make it into a sandwich – easy!

Makes 1 lunch
Prep 10 minutes
Cooking 5 minutes

50g (2oz) podded broad/
  fava beans, fresh
  or frozen

50g (2oz) frozen petits pois

zest and juice of ½ lime,
  plus more to serve
  (optional)

extra-virgin rapeseed oil
  or olive oil

1 slice of sourdough
  or rye bread

1 garlic clove, peeled

chilli flakes, for sprinkling

sea salt and black pepper

Put the broad beans and petits pois in a saucepan of simmering water and cook for 5 minutes. Tip them into a colander and rinse under cold running water to stop them cooking.

Fish out the broad beans, then peel off and discard the skins.

Reserve a few broad beans for decoration, if you like, then put the rest in a blender with the peas, lime zest and juice and about 1 teaspoon of oil. Whizz to combine and roughly chop. Season to taste with salt and pepper.

Toast the bread. While still hot, drizzle it with a little oil and rub the garlic clove over it. Pile the bean mixture on top, add chilli flakes to taste and more lime juice, if you like.

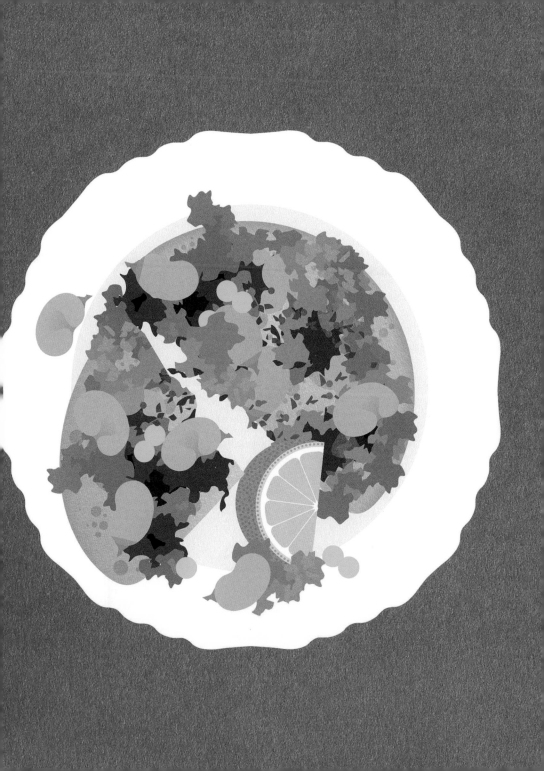

Quick quesadillas

LL

Bored with your usual sandwiches? You can make this quesadilla quickly if working at home, and it's a good one for kids' lunches too. Use any leftover vegetables and beans you have, and opt for seeded wraps for a little extra protein.

Makes 1–2 lunches
Prep 3 minutes
Cooking 5 minutes

1 tsp extra-virgin
    rapeseed oil

2 tortilla wraps

50g (2oz) cheese, grated

75g (3oz) cooked beans
    (red haricot, navy, kidney
    or aduki)

½ small orange or red
    bell pepper, seeded
    and chopped

chilli flakes (optional)

sea salt and black pepper

Heat the oil in a large non-stick frying pan or skillet for a few seconds over a medium heat, then place the first tortilla wrap in the pan.

Sprinkle over about half of the grated cheese, followed by the beans. Sprinkle over the chopped bell pepper, season with salt and pepper and add a few chilli flakes, if using. Cook for 2 minutes, until the cheese starts to melt, then sprinkle over the rest of the cheese. Place the other wrap on top and press it down firmly with a spatula right up the edges. Cook for 1 minute, then carefully turn over the quesadilla. Cook for another 2 minutes, until the underside is browned in most places (lift up using your spatula to check).

Slide the tortilla onto a board and use a pizza wheel or knife to cut it into 6 slices.

Bread

Smashed beetroot, lime and cheese sandwich

FF LL

Beautiful beetroot/beet makes a great sandwich filling. Try to avoid those sold in plastic packaging; the ones sold in glass jars are very good and often cheaper (rinse them first to get rid of some of the vinegar and sugar). Roasting your own is easy too; the key is to prep and roast them when you are cooking something else in order to save on effort and energy. A few chopped walnuts can be used instead of the pumpkin seeds in this tasty sandwich.

Makes 1 lunch
Prep 5 minutes
Cooking 30 minutes (if roasting your own beetroot)

1 fresh beetroot/beet, peeled, or 25g (1oz) cooked beetroot, rinsed and chopped

25g (1oz) crumbly white cheese (dairy or vegan), crumbled

squeeze of lemon or lime juice

1 bagel or chunk of ciabatta, cut in half

handful of rocket/arugula or watercress

1 tsp pumpkin seeds

black pepper

Preheat the oven to 200°C/425°C (if it's not already on for something else).

If using fresh beetroot, cut it into wedges, wrap it in foil and roast for 30 minutes. Test if cooked with the tip of a knife, which should go in easily, then leave to cool.

Put the beetroot and cheese in a blender. Add a squeeze of lemon or lime juice and whizz until smashed but not too smooth. If you don't have a blender, just chop the beetroot finely and mix it in a bowl with the cheese and lemon. Season with black pepper.

Toast the bagel or ciabatta, then fill it with the beetroot mixture, rocket or watercress, and the pumpkin seeds.

— Shop local
Do you tend to buy the same plastic-wrapped packs of cheese all the time? To cut down on food miles and plastic packaging, try cheeses made by local producers. If you love feta, for example, try a locally made salty, crumbly cheese for a change (they are made all over the world, from Yorkshire to Wisconsin). A market stall or cheese store might let you use your own containers, or wrap your purchase in unwaxed paper, if you ask.

Tofu baguettes with radishes, apple and carrot

FF **LL**

If you have any leftover tofu, use it to make this spicy sandwich, which is based on a Vietnamese bánh mì. In Vietnam the tofu would be served hot, which you can do if making this at home, but the sandwich is just as nice cold if you are packing it for work. If you grow your own herbs, add some mint if you have it, but there's no need to buy it specially.

Makes 1 lunch
Prep 5 minutes
Cooking time 8 minutes

1 tsp extra-virgin rapeseed oil or olive oil

50g (2oz) firm smoked tofu, thinly sliced

1 tsp apple cider vinegar

1 tsp chipotle paste or chilli sauce

1 tbsp yoghurt (Greek, plain or coconut)

about 15g fresh coriander/ cilantro

1 small baguette

½ small apple, sliced

1 carrot, peeled and cut into strips or grated

2 radishes, sliced

a few fresh mint leaves (optional)

Heat the oil in a frying pan or skillet over a medium heat. Add the tofu and fry for 5 minutes, then flip and cook for another 3 minutes until the edges are crispy.

Meanwhile, mix together the apple cider vinegar, chipotle paste or chilli sauce and yoghurt in a bowl.

Chop the fresh coriander stems and mix them into the chilli sauce.

Cut the baguette lengthwise, but not all the way through (to stop the filling falling out). Spread the chilli sauce inside.

Fill the baguette with the fried tofu, followed by the apple, carrot and radishes.

Stuff in the coriander leaves and mint leaves, if using. Wrap tightly in wax wrap or foil if taking to work.

Mushroom, leek, aduki bean and miso parcels

LL **NB**

Pastry parcels are a great way to use up whatever vegetables and beans you have in the fridge, and you can add flavour using almost anything – miso, pesto, chilli sauce, fresh or dried herbs, dried fruit … anything you can squeeze in! These are best hot and reheat easily in an oven (a microwave can make the pastry go soft).

Makes 4 parcels
Prep 10 minutes
Cooking 30 minutes

1 tbsp extra-virgin rapeseed oil or olive oil

1 leek, sliced

100g (4oz) mushrooms, chopped

2 tsp red miso paste

200g (7oz) cooked aduki beans

300g (11oz) shortcrust pastry

plain/all-purpose flour, for dusting

milk of your choice, for brushing

black sesame seeds, to garnish (optional)

Preheat the oven to 200°C/425°C (if it's not already on for something else).

Heat the oil in a large pan over a medium heat, add the leek and mushrooms and cook for 5 minutes until the leeks have softened. Add the miso paste and beans and stir well until the paste has dissolved.

Roll out the pastry on a floured surface to a thickness of about 3mm (¼in). Cut the pastry into 4 squares, each about 15 x 15cm (6 x 6in).

Spoon the bean mixture into the centre of each square and spread it out a little.

Brush the edges with a little milk. Bring the corners of each square into the centre and pinch together to seal. Brush over a little more milk. Sprinkle over a few black sesame seeds for decoration, if you like. Place on a baking tray lined with baking paper (or use a non-stick tray) and bake in the oven for 25 minutes, until the pastry is golden brown.

— Love your leftovers
Black beans, kidney beans and chickpeas all work well in parcels too, so if you have a few left over, don't throw them away – freeze them for when you want to make some parcels. Just add a few vegetables (sweetcorn and bell peppers are great), and a little pasta sauce, salsa or pesto, and get inventive with your leftovers!

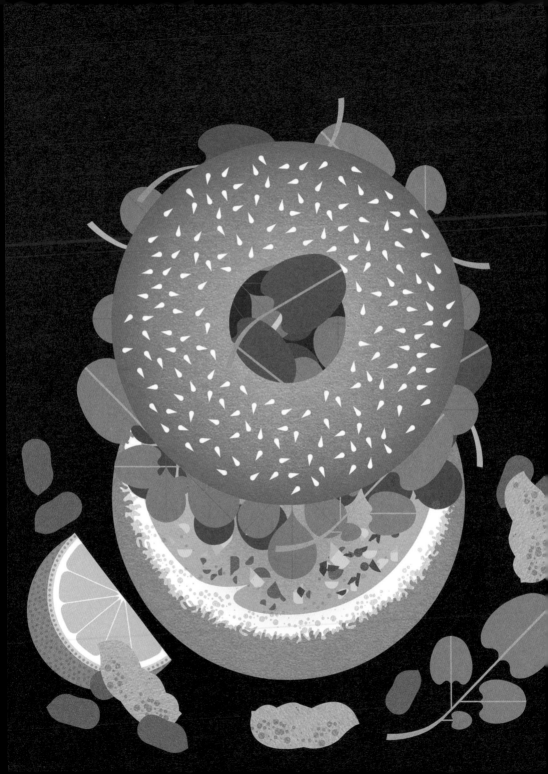

Peanut butter, lime, chilli and watercress bagel

(5)

Here's a quick, protein-packed bagel for when you need a change from your regular sandwiches. Peanut butter goes well with salad, so if you tend to eat it just on its own on toast, why not give this a go?

Makes 1 lunch
Prep 2 minutes
Cooking 2 minutes

1 bagel, cut in half
1 tbsp chunky peanut butter
lime wedge
a few chilli flakes
handful of watercress

Pop your bagel in the toaster.

Spread one half with the peanut butter, add a squeeze of lime juice and a few chilli flakes. Add watercress, and sandwich together.

— Mix it up
You can swap watercress for rocket/arugula or spinach leaves, or whatever you have available – all dark green salad leaves are packed with nutrients.

Mix and match sandwiches

5 NB

Many of us get into the habit of making or buying the same sandwiches day in, day out. And, let's be honest, do you really think all the packaging for bought sandwiches gets recycled? Many of the veggie sandwiches for sale have huge mark-ups too, so if you can get into the habit of making your own now and then,

BREADS	+	PROTEINS
Hearty homemade or bakery bread is so much more satisfying than regular sliced sandwich bread. Why not buy (or bake) an interesting loaf at the weekend, cut it into slices and freeze it, ready to make a truly delicious sandwich midweek? Here are a few ideas to remind you of just some of the amazing variety of breads available.		To avoid mid-afternoon energy slumps, you need some protein in your sandwich. You don't need me to tell you about cheese and hummus, so how about some of these fillings instead?

rye
pumpernickel
seeded
granary
walnut and raisin
chia and linseed
ciabatta
baguette
focaccia
olive
naan
roti
flatbreads
tortilla
pitta
cholla
soda
bagels

edamame beans
peas
butter/lima beans
kidney beans
cannellini beans
tofu (smoked, sliced, scrambled…)
falafel
chickpeas
chuna (see page 93)
nut butters (peanut, almond, cashew…)
pine nuts
yoghurt/tzatziki

you can spend your cash on better, more delicious ingredients, and get more variety and nutrients into your day.

Pick and mix something from each group below to make your perfect sandwich!

VEGETABLES AND FRUITS + EXTRAS

Something with crunch works well in a sandwich. Those old classics, cucumber and tomato, can make bread soggy, so why not try something new? Cram as many veggies as you can into each sandwich and mix it up each day.

Pop in some extra flavour to take your sandwich to the next level. You might have some of the items below knocking around in the kitchen already – you only need a little for a flavour hit.

cress
beetroot/beet mash (see page 27)
carrot
watercress
rocket/arugula
red bell pepper
tomatoes (fresh, sun-dried, roasted...)
sugar snap peas
kale (blitzed)
peas
red cabbage (fresh or pickled)
sauerkraut
kimchi
roast vegetables
slaw (see pages 40–1)
apple
satsuma
apricots
sultanas

olives
fresh herbs
pickles
pesto
homemade chutney
chilli (dried flakes or freshly chopped)
capers
mustard
harissa paste
pumpkin seeds
sesame seeds

Charred sweetcorn patties

NB

Thai-style curry pastes are an easy way to add a quick hit of ginger, lemongrass and chilli into your everyday lunches (you can buy them without fish sauce in). Eat these patties with salad and a squeeze of lime juice, or in burger buns or ciabatta with slaw for a more substantial lunch.

Makes 3–4 lunches (8 patties)
Prep 10 minutes
Cooking 10–15 minutes
(depending on pan size)

**2 corn on the cobs, or
    300g/11oz canned
    or frozen sweetcorn
    kernels**

**2 spring onions/scallions,
    chopped**

2 eggs, lightly beaten

**100g (4oz/¾ cup)
    self-raising flour**

**1 tbsp Thai red curry
    paste**

extra-virgin rapeseed oil

sea salt and black pepper

To serve

**burger buns or ciabatta
    (optional)**

**salad or slaw of choice
    (see pages 40–1)**

If using fresh corn, strip the kernels from the cobs using a sharp knife. Heat a large frying pan or skillet (there is no need for any oil) over a medium–high heat, add the corn kernels and spring onions and cook for 5 minutes until the kernels char at the edges.

Put the eggs and flour in a blender. Add about half the charred sweetcorn mixture and whizz until fairly smooth. Spoon it into a bowl, add the rest of the sweetcorn mixture plus the Thai red curry paste and stir well. Season with salt and pepper.

Put a little oil in the pan and place over a medium heat. When hot, add 2 or 3 separate heaped tablespoons of the patty mixture (the number depends on how many you can fit in your pan). Cook for 2 minutes, then flip them over and cook for a further 2 minutes. Remove from the pan and repeat with the rest of the mixture to make 8 patties.

If you're taking this lunch to work, take salad or a pot of slaw with you, and a burger bun or piece of ciabatta, if you like. The patties are nice hot or cold. You can also assemble a burger/sandwich before work – just wrap it up tightly so it doesn't fall apart on the move.

— Eat seasonal
Fresh corn in season is delicious and often pretty cheap. If you have lots of corn cobs, you can strip off the kernels and freeze them for later in the year. Sweetcorn kernels in cans (not creamed) will also work for patties, so you can eat this lunch all year round.

Bread

Black bean patties with avocado and radish salsa

(W) (NB)

Black bean patties make a great change from falafel. The mint adds a delicious freshness, but you can also use coriander/cilantro. Stuff the patties into pitta breads or burger buns, whichever you prefer.

Makes 3–6 lunches (6 patties)
Prep 10 minutes
Cooking 10 minutes

1 x 400g (14oz) can black
   beans, drained
1 slice of bread (about
   50g/2oz)
1 tsp chipotle paste
1 small onion, peeled and
   finely chopped
handful of fresh mint,
   chopped
1 egg
2 tbsp extra-virgin
   rapeseed oil
sea salt and black pepper

To serve

1 avocado, peeled, stoned
   and chopped
3–4 radishes, chopped
zest and juice of 1 lime
3–6 pitta breads or
   burger buns

Put the beans in a blender and whizz until some are mashed and some are still whole. Tip them out and set aside.

Put the bread in the blender and whizz to make breadcrumbs.

Put the beans, breadcrumbs, chipotle paste, onion, mint and egg in a bowl and mix well. Season with salt and pepper.

Divide the mixture into 6 equal pieces. Roll each piece into a ball, then press gently to flatten into a circle, about 6cm (2½in) in diameter.

Heat the oil in a large non-stick frying pan or skillet over a medium heat. Place three patties in the pan and cook for 4 minutes. Gently turn them over and cook for another 3 minutes until browned. Place on some kitchen paper. Cook the remaining three patties.

Meanwhile, put the avocado, radishes, lime zest and juice in a bowl and mix well. Season with salt and pepper.

If taking this lunch to work, pack the bread and avocado salsa separately. Reheat the patties if you like, but they are nice hot or cold. You can also assemble a pitta or burger before work – just wrap it up tightly so it doesn't fall apart on the move.

— Making breadcrumbs
There is no need to buy plastic packets of breadcrumbs. Just whizz fresh or stale bread in a blender to make your own and freeze until you need them. Any bread will work – white, granary, wholewheat, ciabatta, sourdough …

Smoky pulled jackfruit bun with carrot and sesame seed slaw

W NB

Jackfruit is now widely available in cans; it's a great ingredient to have to hand if you don't want to eat meat and people in your household miss it. It's delicious hot, so this is a good option for a weekend lunch. The pulled jackfruit freezes well, so if you don't need all the portions at once, just put any leftovers in the freezer.

Makes 4 lunches
Prep 5 minutes
Cooking 30 minutes

1 tbsp extra-virgin rapeseed oil or olive oil

1 small red onion, peeled and thinly sliced

1 garlic clove, peeled and chopped

1 tbsp smoked paprika

1 tsp brown or white sugar

200g (7oz) canned chopped tomatoes

1 x 400g (14oz) can green/young jackfruit pieces in salted water

1 tsp chilli flakes

4 brioche or burger buns, or pieces of ciabatta

black pepper

watercress or spinach leaves, to serve

For the carrot and sesame seed slaw

2 carrots, peeled and grated

1 tsp black sesame seeds

zest and juice of 1 lime

Heat the oil in a frying pan or skillet over a very low heat. When hot, add the onion and garlic, put the lid on and cook for 10 minutes until the onion has softened.

Add the paprika, sugar and tomatoes and stir, then add the jackfruit, along with the water from the can. Bring to a simmer, then reduce the heat and cook for 15 minutes. Break up the jackfruit using a wooden spoon and stir well. Continue to cook for another 5 minutes. Add the chilli flakes and black pepper to taste (there is no need to add salt).

Meanwhile, combine all the slaw ingredients in a bowl and mix well.

Toast the buns or ciabatta lightly, then fill with leaves, warm jackfruit and slaw.

Bread

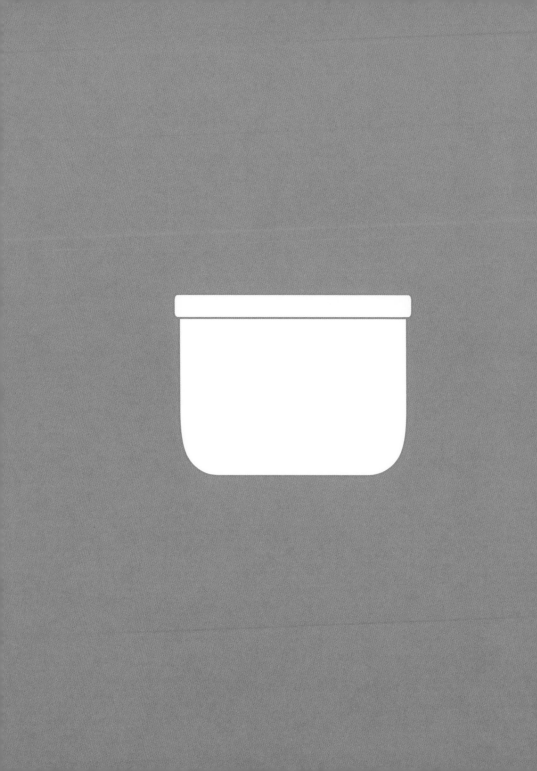

Snacks

Carrot cake bliss balls

5 **LL**

These are so quick and easy to make and much more eco-friendly than buying snack balls wrapped in single-use plastic. Store them in the fridge at work or at home (they will keep well in an airtight container for at least a week) and munch them whenever you need an energy boost.

Makes 6 balls
Prep 5 minutes

50g (2oz) walnuts (broken or halves are fine)

75g (3oz) dates, chopped

1 small carrot, peeled and finely grated

½ tsp mixed spice or ground cinnamon

a little lemon zest

Put everything in a blender and whizz to combine. Don't worry if the dates and walnuts are still a little chunky.

Roll the mixture into six balls using your hands.

Put them in the fridge to firm up, and store there until you're ready to eat.

— Other things to put in/on your bliss balls

You can use up all sorts of things in your cupboards to make bliss balls, as you need only small amounts (halve the quantities listed if you want to experiment). Why not try peanuts, macadamias, almonds, pistachios, nut butters, dried apricots, cherries and figs, raspberries, cacao, coconut or chia seeds? You can also roll the balls in coatings such as desiccated coconut, matcha powder or cacao powder. Just have a go!

Snacks

Blackberry, banana and lemon buns

LL **W**

Overripe bananas and soft fruits are often thrown away, so if you have some looking slightly past their best, try this easy bake. I make these when we have picked wild blackberries, but you can also use fresh or frozen raspberries, blueberries, gooseberries or blackcurrants instead. Dried fruits, such as sultanas, apricots, cranberries, sour cherries or figs, also work really well. These buns make a nice work breakfast or mid-afternoon snack.

Makes 6 buns
Prep 12 minutes
Cooking 20–25 minutes

50ml (3 tablespoons) milk of your choice

zest and juice of ½ lemon

50g (2oz) butter or vegan block butter, plus extra for greasing

125g (5oz/1 cup) self-raising flour

50g (2oz/¼ cup) caster/superfine sugar

1 overripe banana, mashed

1 egg

50g (2oz) blackberries

poppy seeds, for sprinkling (optional)

Put the milk, lemon zest and juice in a bowl and stir. Leave for 10 minutes while you get on with the next steps.

Preheat the oven to 180°C/400°F (if it's not already on for something else). Line a 6-hole muffin tray with paper cases, or, if using a silicone tray, rub a little extra butter inside.

Melt the butter in a small pan over a low heat, then leave to cool a little.

Sift the flour into a mixing bowl and add the sugar. Pour in the melted butter and add the mashed banana.

Break the egg into the milk mixture and give it a stir to break it up. Add this to the flour mixture. Add the blackberries and mix until evenly combined.

Spoon the mixture into the muffin tray and sprinkle over the poppy seeds, if using. Bake for 20–25 minutes until lightly golden on top.

— Bananas

If your bananas often go brown before you get a chance to eat them, make a point of freezing them sooner for use in baking and smoothies. Peel and chop up, pop in a container or bag and put in the freezer. Defrost before baking, or use frozen for smoothies.

Snacks

Sweet and salty popcorn

NB **5**

Love popcorn? Making your own is very easy and cheap, so you won't need to buy packets of ready-made. Have a bag in your desk for when you need a snack between meetings, or if you need something for a long commute home. Reuse any food bags you already have before investing in eco reusable bags (look for products made with recycled materials). Wipe out or wash bags between uses and aim to get as many uses out of each one as possible. You can also use tins and plastic tubs, but they will be bulkier to transport.

Makes 2 bags
Cooking 5 minutes

1 tbsp extra-virgin
   rapeseed oil
50g (2oz) popping corn
2 tbsp butter or coconut oil
1 tbsp honey or golden
   syrup
sea salt

Use a large non-stick saucepan, ideally one with a see-through lid. Add the oil and place the pan over a medium heat.

Once the oil is hot, add the corn, give the pan a shake to coat the kernels in the oil, and put the lid on. Leave for a minute over a high heat, then, when the kernels start to pop, turn the heat down low.

The corn will take just 2–3 minutes to pop, so don't leave it unattended. Make sure to give the pan a shake now and then. As soon as the sound of popping has pretty much stopped, remove the pan from the heat so the popped kernels don't burn. Leave for a minute or two with the lid on, as a few more kernels may pop.

Tip the popcorn into a bowl and remove any unpopped kernels.

Put the butter or coconut oil in the pan and heat until melted. Add the honey or golden syrup and stir until combined. Add the popcorn and stir to coat. Add sea salt to taste.

— Dark chocolate popcorn
Melt 25g (1oz) of dark/semisweet chocolate in a non-stick pan, then tip in your popped corn. Remove from the heat and stir until coated.

— Paprika popcorn
When you melt the butter or coconut oil, stir in 1 tsp smoked paprika instead of the honey or golden syrup.

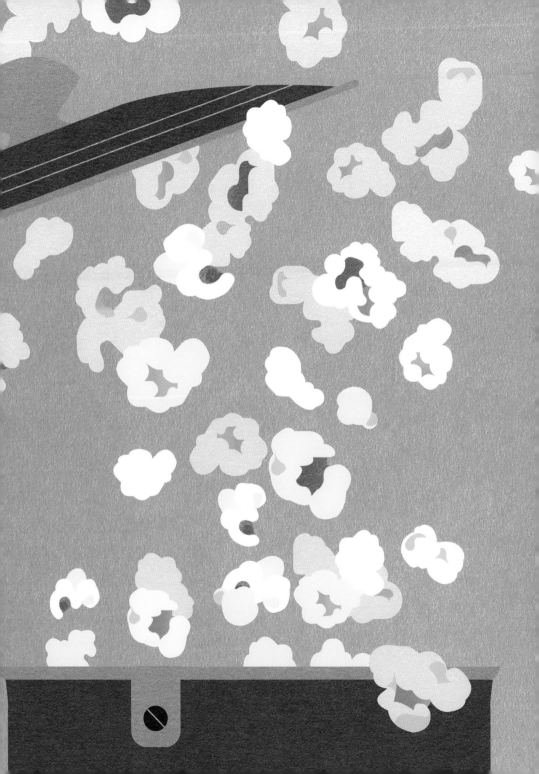

Lime and tamari kale crisps

(LL) (NB)

Kale always seems to come in large amounts, so this is a great way to use it all up. The tamari and lime add a delicious umami flavour, and these crisps are lovely with sandwiches or as a mid-afternoon snack. Cavolo nero and curly kale both make good crisps.

Makes 1 bag
Prep 2 minutes
Cooking 25 minutes

50g (2oz) trimmed kale

1 tsp extra-virgin rapeseed oil or olive oil

zest and juice of ½ lime

1 tsp tamari or soy sauce

sea salt (optional)

Preheat the oven to 100°C/250°F.

Snip the kale leaves into small pieces, all about the same size, using scissors.

Put the kale, oil, lime zest and juice, tamari or soy sauce in a large bowl and massage together with your hands to coat the leaves thoroughly. This sounds odd but it works better than using a spoon!

Spread out the kale in a large baking tray and roast for 25 minutes, until crisp but still green. Remove from the oven and leave to cool.

Snacks

Spicy nuts and seeds

(LL)

This is a great way to give new life to any stray nuts in almost-empty packets, or any that are turning soft. Munch them for a snack, or chop them up and sprinkle in salads.

Makes 2 snacks
Prep 2 minutes
Cooking 15 minutes

50g (2oz) nuts
(e.g. macadamias,
almonds, walnuts)

1 tsp pumpkin seeds

1 tsp extra-virgin rapeseed
oil or olive oil

1 tsp smoked paprika

½ tsp ground cumin

½ tsp honey or golden
syrup

sea salt and black pepper

Preheat the oven to 160°C/350°F (if it's not already on for something else).

Put all the ingredients together in a bowl, season with salt and pepper and stir.

Line a roasting tray with baking paper and spread out the nuts and seeds. Roast for 15 minutes, then remove from the oven and leave to cool. Store in a jam jar or tin.

Flexi-flapjack bars

W **NB**

It's so tempting to pick up a plastic-wrapped flapjack or cake when buying coffee or sandwiches, but all those little plastic packets add up, in cost as well as plastic footprint. This recipe is all about flexibility; use your favourite dried fruits, nuts and seeds to make flapjacks exactly as you like. These bars are a good commuting breakfast or an energy-boosting afternoon snack.

Makes 6 bars
Prep 5 minutes
Cooking 15–20 minutes

50g (2oz) butter or vegan block butter

50g (2 oz/scant ¼ cup) brown sugar

1 tbsp golden syrup

100g (4oz) oats

75g (3oz) dried apricots, chopped

1 tsp chia seeds

1 tbsp almonds, chopped

Preheat the oven to 160°C/350°F (if it's not already on for something else) and line a small baking tray (about 18 x 12cm/7 x 5in) with baking paper. (If you don't have exactly the right tin, don't rush out and buy one. A shallow round cake tin will also work, or use a larger tray and just fill one side to about 1cm/½in deep.)

Put the butter, sugar and syrup in a small saucepan and heat until melted, then add the oats, apricots, chia seeds and almonds and stir well. Tip the mixture into the prepared tin and press it into the edges.

Bake for 15–20 minutes, until golden on top. Leave to cool for 5 minutes, then cut into 6 flapjacks (still in the tin as the mixture will be crumbly at this stage). Leave to cool completely before lifting out.

— Other things to put in your flapjacks

Swap the apricots for: sultanas, raisins, dates, dried cranberries, mango, figs, apple or cherries.

Swap the chia seeds for: sesame seeds, linseeds, sunflower seeds or pumpkin seeds.

Swap the almonds for: hazelnuts, macadamias, walnuts, pistachios, brazil nuts or peanuts.

Graze boxes

(5) (LL)

This isn't a recipe as such – more ideas on how to up your snack game and ditch single-use packaging. Find a great container that has a tight-fitting lid, then fill it with snacks to keep you going through the working day. Refill stores are great sources of nuts, dried fruit, chocolate buttons and more.

Below are some suggestions for things you can mix and match in your graze box. If you have a small bento box, you can keep everything separate, but I don't mind letting things mix together in my container for a salty and sweet combo!

— Macadamias
— Peanuts
— Cashews
— Almonds
— Brazil nuts
— Pistachios

— Apricots
— Cranberries
— Sour cherries
— Apple rings
— Pineapple
— Sultanas
— Banana chips

— Yoghurt-coated raisins
— Dark chocolate squares
  and buttons

— Roasted broad/fava beans
— Roasted yellow peas
— Roasted chickpeas

— Pumpkin seeds

— Popcorn (see page 124)
— Breadsticks
— Crackers
— Pretzels

Super seed crackers

(W)

Seeds are a great source of protein and healthy fats. These baked crackers are easy to make and include pumpkin seeds, chia seeds and sesame seeds. Eat them on their own or with no-sesame hummus or chuna (see pages 92 and 93), or any other dip you like.

Makes 12 crackers
Prep 5 minutes
Cooking 1 hour

50g (2oz) quinoa
25g (1oz) chia seeds
2 tbsp pumpkin seeds
2 tbsp sesame seeds
1 tsp chilli flakes
sea salt and black pepper

Preheat the oven to 160°C/350°F (if it's not already on for something else) and line a 24 x 18cm (9½ x 7in) baking sheet with baking paper.

Meanwhile, cook the quinoa for 20 minutes in a pan of simmering water. When cooked, drain and leave to cool.

Meanwhile, put the chia seeds in a heatproof bowl, pour over 75ml (5 tablespoons) boiling water and stir.

When the quinoa is cooked, stir in the chia seeds, pumpkin seeds, sesame seeds and chilli flakes, then add plenty of salt and pepper.

Spread the mixture onto the prepared tray and smooth it out to a thickness of about 3mm. Bake for 25 minutes.

Remove the tray from the oven and cut the cracker sheet into 12 squares. Turn each cracker over carefully, and return the tray to the oven for 15 minutes until golden. Remove and leave to cool. The crackers will keep for about a week in an airtight container.

Snacks

Veg box crisps

You can make vegetable crisps from pretty much any root vegetable, so if you have a couple in your veg box that are softening and you are not sure what to do with them, give this recipe a go. The crisps are lovely with sandwiches, or any time you need a snack. Just pop them in the oven when you are cooking something else. Take to work in a container or reusable bag.

Makes 2 bags
Prep 5 minutes
Cooking 10–15 minutes

1 parsnip

1 sweet potato

1 white potato

1 large carrot

3 tbsp extra-virgin rapeseed oil or olive oil

1 tsp smoked paprika

sea salt

Preheat the oven to 200°C/425°F (if it's not already on for something else).

To prep your vegetables, peel or scrub them, then slice very thinly (the thinner the better), using a mandoline or very sharp knife.

Place the vegetables in a single layer on two large non-stick baking trays. Mix together the oil and paprika. Brush the vegetable slices with the mixture. Flip them over and brush again.

Bake for 10 minutes, then remove any smaller crisps that are turning brown. Continue to bake any thicker crisps for a further 5 minutes.

Remove from the oven and season with plenty of sea salt. Leave to cool before eating. These crisps are best eaten the same day.

— Mixing it up
Beetroot/beet and turnips also make good crisps. You can skip the paprika and season with chilli or black pepper if you prefer.

Snacks

Index by symbol

General index

The centigrade temperature given in the recipes is for a fan oven. Here are some helpful conversions.

	Electricity °C	Electricity (fan) °C	Electricity °F	Gas Mark
Very cool	110	90	225	¼
	120	100	250	½
Cool	140	120	275	1
	150	130	300	2
Moderate	160	140	325	3
	180	160	350	4
Moderately hot	190	170	375	5
	200	180	400	6
Hot	220	200	425	7
	230	210	450	8
Very hot	240	220	475	9

Acknowledgements

My move to eating mostly plant foods each day has taken a few years, and there are lots of fab people who have helped me along the way, with ideas and gentle inspiration. Thank you to Michelle Lake for sharing her knowledge of eating a balanced, nutritious menu. To Marianne Jordan for introducing me to vegan cakes and nut roast many years ago and for Ethical Fridays. Thank you also to Anne Harvey aka Taste of Vietnam for her tips on making banh mi (apologies for my non-authentic version.). To Helen Ross for telling me what it's like taking vegan lunches to sixth form and sharing her excellent top tips. To Sancha for her USA cheese knowledge. Thank you to Katie, Alex and Dani for invaluable expert input! Thanks also to the Sustainable St Albans team who inspire us all by bringing together food makers and eco-warriors so we can all learn new things (and change). Thank you to Barrie Johnston and the Great in 8 gang who were endlessly supportive, telling me which lunches they liked most, which they took to work and which got the most 'oooohs' from colleagues. I also loved hearing from everyone who bought and used *Packed*, including many wonderful photos; I hope you find new things to enjoy in here.

A huge thank you to Zoe Ross at United Agents who saw what this book could be, over matching bowls of porridge one freezing morning. Thank you also to The Guild of Food Writers for hosting the event where I first met Zoe, and for being a generous group of talented foodies. A big thank you to Elen Jones and Laurence King for totally getting this book and for choosing it to be your first LK cookery book – what an honour! To Andrew for bringing fresh eyes and ideas. Sally Caulwell's illustrations are works of art and I am so fortunate to see my recipes brought to life in such a beautiful way. Thank you to Issy, Emily and their creative team for the beautiful food photography and styling. Thanks to Laura Nickoll and Patricia Burgess for their valuable editorial input and Marie Lorimer for the index.

And finally thanks to Steve for testing pretty much every recipe, often more than once, and for being my work-at-home buddy.

Index

First published in Great Britain in 2022 by Laurence King Publishing
an imprint of The Orion Publishing Group Ltd
Carmelite House, 50 Victoria Embankment
London EC4Y 0DZ

An Hachette UK Company

10 9 8 7 6 5 4 3 2

A CIP catalogue record for this book is available from the British Library.

ISBN 978 1 913 94786 6

Origination by F1 Colour Ltd, London
Printed in China by C&C Offset Printing Co. Ltd.

Laurence King Publishing is committed to ethical and sustainable
production. We are proud participants in the The Book Chain Project®
bookchainproject.com

www.laurenceking.com
www.orionbooks.co.uk